INDIAN BIRDS IN FOCUS

Birds of the Indian subcontinent and their Habitats

Photography and Text
Amano Samarpan

wisdom
tree

"Man has become too serious, has lost his playfulness,
has become so knowlegeable he has lost his innocence.
Hence it is better to mix with other species:
birds and fish, other animals and trees,
to have the whole universe as your commune,
not just human beings who have gone too astray..."

– Osho

ISBN 978-81-8328-138-6

Published by
Wisdom Tree,
4779/23, Ansari Road,
Darya Ganj, New Delhi-2
Ph.: 23247966/67/68
wisdomtree@vsnl.com

Printed in India at Print Perfect

(*Previous page*) A male chestnut-bellied sandgrouse (*Pterocles exustus*) having flown to a nearby pool to wet its breast feathers now allows a chick who cannot yet make the journey, to sip the moisture without which the fledgling would soon die in the sometimes harsh environment it inhabits.

(*Opposite*) Wedge-tailed green pigeon (*Treron sphenurus*) in a tree near the fast flowing Mandakini River, Uttarakhand.

CONTENTS

View of the Ramnagar River and Himalayan foothills near Dhikala, Corbett National Park.

INTRODUCTION

Ornithology has many different ways to classify birds. These can be according to size and colouration, body shape and parts, sex and age, breeding cycle and nesting activity, voice and possible migratory patterns while yet another factor for consideration is the kind of habitat a bird might favour. Birds typically have evolved through their ability to exploit a certain ecological niche. Although the environment a particular bird prefers over another is seldom a defining characteristic, such classification can help in identifying birds in the field and provide valuable data towards understanding their behaviour.

Most birds will depend upon more than one habitat. For instance, the tawny fish owl (*Ketupa flavipes*) needs to be in reach of a sizeable water body such as a river or lake to fish, yet lives and breeds in the seclusion of the forest.

Birds such as the Eurasian wryneck(*Jynx torquilla*) regularly visit different habitats including woodland, grassland, scrub and semi-desert. On the other hand, there are birds more reliant on a particular environment such as the common snipe (*Gallinago gallinago*) whose specific colouration enables them to blend almost seamlessly into their habitat.

Different habitats overlap while they can also be contained in each other. For instance, a swamp could be a grassland in water while one finds deserts in mountains; water bodies in deserts as well as in forests. This diversity does not detract from the value habitat plays in species recognition. Warblers, for example, are a large group of small birds often rather dull looking and difficult to differentiate between and so identify correctly. The fact that some prefer scrub or grassland while others prefer woodland, can assist in identifying them. For instance, two of the more common warblers of the Indian subcontinent can be separated by their relationship to water; the clamorous reed warbler (*Acrocephalus stentoreus*) is found close to water while the Blyth's reed warbler (*Acrocephalus dumetorum*) lives at a distance from water and in a drier habitat.

There are also migrating birds such as the ruddy shelduck (*Tadorna ferruginea*) which prefer lakes and slow moving rivers as their habitat. In summer, they take off for the Himalayan mountains to breed where they will choose a similar habitat. Here however, the emphasis will be on finding a place that also offers a suitable nesting site as well as plentiful source of food.

Classification of the various habitats identified in this book do not conform to any particular module as there is not a generally recognised one. There exist a complex number of ecological communities which are not easily typecast into a few; nevertheless, the classification here is readily understandable and in common parlance.

A tawny fish owl (*Ketupa flavipes*) roosting in forest near the Ramnagar River of Corbett National Park.

Amidst fishponds near Kolkata, a common snipe (*Gallinago gallinago*)
blends into the background vegetation.

(*Opposite*) Eurasian wryneck (*Jynx torquilla*)
on the outskirts of Gurgaon in Haryana.

(*Pages 6 to 7*) Ruddy shelduck *(Tadorna ferruginea)*
drift along the waters of the Mulla River in Pune, Maharashtra.

Blyth's reed warbler (*Acrocephalus dumetorum*) in the hills of southern Orissa.

A clamorous reed warbler (*Acrocephalus stentoreus*) on the banks of the Yamuna River in Delhi.

BIRDS OF THE WATER

Where there is water there is life; this is certainly true in the world of birds.

A western osprey (*Pandion haliaetus*) having caught a fish from a nearby pool close to the Manas National Park in Assam needs to fend off other raptors; eventually it flew off to eat its meal in the seclusion of nearby woodland.

All birds need water, yet for some it plays an essential part in their day-to-day life and they may actually spend much of their time in the water even nesting very close to it.

Geese such as the bar-headed goose (*Anser indicus*) frequent water bodies although they often find their food on farmland; like the ruddy shelduck, they are migrants who spend the warmer months in the heights of the Himalayas.

Water itself is life-giving and supports a mass of organisms many of which are a potential source of food to birds. The most obvious of these are fish and some birds have developed the ability to catch them. This includes a number of raptors, large birds of prey, that can lift a fish out of the water with their talons as they fly low over the surface. The western osprey (*Pandion haliaetus*) is a striking example, as it hurtles from the sky to hit the water with a loud splash, grabbing for the fish with an outstretched claw. For a moment or two, it may float on the water before flying off, perhaps slowly at first since if it has been successful, it needs to secure its struggling victim. Birds such as the vulnerable Pallas's fish eagle (*Haliaeetus leucoryphus*) and the near threatened grey-headed fish eagle (*Ichthyophaga ichthyaetus)* perch from where they can see fish moving in the waters below, before launching their attack.

Some birds swim to catch their prey. Among these is the vulnerable spot-billed pelican (*Pelecanus philippensis*) that in the final moment will leap out of the water before pouncing to surprise its victim. The near threatened oriental darter (*Anhinga melanogaster*) will swim underwater to catch its prey sometimes to suddenly emerge above the surface with a fish speared in its beak; it will also toss a fish up in the air before consuming it head first.

The kingfishers, of which there are a dozen major species in the Indian subcontinent, are impressive birds in both colour and voice as well as being very skillful at fishing. The white-throated kingfisher (*Halcyon smyrensis*) fishes not only in water bodies such as ponds and rivers but also in puddles, taking a variety of prey that includes fish, insects, lizards, young birds and even mice; it has not become as adept a hunter though as the pied kingfisher (*Ceryle rudis*) which can be seen over water, hovering high in the air for sometime, before dropping like a stone to seize prey underwater.

There are many varieties of duck in India, most of which are winter visitors and some of them can be seen in their hundreds. The Indian spot-billed duck (*Anas poecilorhyncha*) is a resident species seen throughout the year where enough water is to be found. The little cormorant (*Phalacrocorax niger*) is another bird seen perching in the vicinity of water; it swims and dives for fish.

Waterbirds depend on water for their livelihood and when water gets polluted, a common occurrence in the highly industrialised world of today, such birds are forced to go elsewhere or suffer like their prey often do.

(Previous pages)
A group of bar-headed geese (*Anser indicus*) on the waters of a lake in the Sariska National Park of northern Rajasthan.

A Pallas's fish eagle (*Haliaeetus leucoryphus*) soars high over the Kaziranga National Park in Assam.

(*Opposite*) Not far from the main entrance of Kaziranga, a grey-headed fish eagle (*Ichthyophaga ichthyaetus*) pauses with its recently caught fish secured by the talons of one foot, alert to chattering tourists passing nearby who remain oblivious of the bird's presence.

A spot-billed pelican (*Pelecanus philippensis*) leaps to pounce on unsuspecting fish in a river to the east of Kaziranga National Park.

(*Opposite*) In a large pond at the Keoladeo National Park in Rajasthan, an oriental darter (*Anhinga melanogaster*) having dived to catch a fish now tosses it up before swallowing the small creature head first.

(*Above*) A white-throated kingfisher (*Halcyon smyrensis*) perches on a plant; it can find food even around puddles of water, yet (*Opposite*) the pied kingfisher (*Ceryle rudis*) seen here hovering over a river in Rajasthan, needs a substantial water body in which to fish.

A pair of immature Indian spot-billed duck (*Anas poecilorhyncha*) navigate a pool in Delhi Zoo.

(*Opposite*) A little cormorant (*Phalacrocorax niger*) perches in the middle of the Yamuna River.

BIRDS OF THE SHORELINE

Many birds come to the water's edge to drink yet some also find their food there and can frequently be seen in the vicinity. Among these are the waders, so called because they forage as they walk in water, while some birds find nourishment not just in the shallower waters but also along the higher shoreline where many other edible creatures are to be found.

A number of herons are found in the region and can be seen at the water's edge. Although the grey heron (*Ardea cinerea*) is typically seen in swampland, it is often at the edge of water bodies, standing still and silent for long periods before suddenly stabbing into the water with their long dagger shaped bills to secure prey. The more solitary striated heron (*Butorides striatus*) has similar habits and both species sometimes nest and roost in trees.

The demoiselle crane (*Anthropoides virgo*), a winter visitor to India, is attracted to water bodies such as rivers and ponds although it can be found feeding among winter crops and in stubble fields during the day.

The sandpipers (*Tringa*), a family that includes the redshanks, are medium sized birds that wander along shorelines. The common redshank (*Tringa totanus*) is more solitary, picking at the ground as it goes while the wood sandpiper (*Tringa glareola*) feeds on creatures found in mud and is often seen moving in a small group.

A bird such as the black-headed gull (*Larus ridibundus*) is usually found at the water's edge both along the coast and inland yet, can also be seen in fields and following ships out at sea.

The black-winged stilt (*Himantopus himantopus*) is a gregarious yet graceful wader that finds its invertebrate food both in and out of the water as it stealthily and deliberately walks along. Pied avocet (*Recurvirostra avosetta*) also gregarious by nature, feed when wading through water; they sweep their bill from side to side occasionally submerging their heads to take prey.

The little ringed plover (*Charadrius dubius*) is another wader that can sometimes be seen vibrating a suspended foot around wet mud as it searches for food along the water's edge, though it may also be seen in wet grassland and in paddyfields. The small pratincole (*Glareola lactea*) although found along the shoreline, usually on the banks of shingle or sand of inland waters, finds its food by flying low over the water and hawking insects.

Shorelines however are being threatened as human beings also like to be close to water. Mojim Beach in Goa where some of the birds seen here were photographed, is experiencing increased pressure from tourism as shacks appear on the beach and more pedestrians take to the sands; the birds that have been coming here for hundreds of years may need to go elsewhere.

With lightning response, a striated heron (*Butorides striatus*) takes a small fish from one of Goa's many inland waterways.

(*Previous pages*) A grey heron (*Ardea cinerea*) wades through a pond in Rajasthan with its catch.

A couple of demoiselle cranes (*Anthropoides virgo*) drink quietly by a pool outside Khichan village in Rajasthan.

(*Opposite*)
A common redshank
(*Tringa totanus*)
preening in the twilight.

A wood sandpiper (*Tringa glareola*) pauses for a moment while searching for food alongside a pool in Haryana.

(*Opposite*) A small group of black-headed gulls on Mojim Beach in Goa.

A pied avocet (*Recurvirostra avosetta*) wades through a shallow pool in Haryana.

(*Opposite*) An immature black-winged stilt (*Himantopus himantopus*) wading along a stream near the Yamuna River.

A little ringed plover (*Charadrius dubius*) walks over the sandy banks
of the Koshi River in southern Nepal.

(*Opposite*) A small pratincole (*Glareola lactea*) roosts on a beach in northern Goa;
its confident stance may result from it being part of a flock of a dozen or so birds.

BIRDS OF THE SWAMP

Swamp is an area of waterlogged ground splendidly rich in biodiversity.

Swamp is a term used to describe waterlogged areas that may contain streams and ponds but are largely covered in vegetation, so much so that in some cases the area can be described as moist grassland.

The vulnerable yet graceful Indian or sarus crane (*Grus antigone*) prefers a habitat that is flooded or partially flooded although it can also be seen in drier areas such as on ploughed fields.

The endangered greater adjutant stork (*Leptoptilos dubius*) is a large bird sometimes found near human habitation; its preferred natural habitat is swampy ground although as a scavenger it will also be found on refuse tips.

The vulnerable greater spotted eagle (*Aquila clanga*) is a large raptor that hunts small amphibians as well as mammals; it will also take other birds including ducks, even working with others of its kind to achieve this end. Another though smaller bird of prey that hunts by flying low over marshes is known as the western marsh harrier (*Circus aeruginosus*) which will supplement its diet by pirating prey from other raptors. Although not waterbirds, both species find a valuable food supply amidst the swamp.

Life for the purple swamphen (*Porphyrio porphyrio)* is mostly spent wandering through floating vegetation and reeds although it also swims occasionally; while feeding on the pith of reeds which are ripped apart, the bird uses its beak and a claw to secure the stem. The white-breasted waterhen (*Amaurornis phoenicurus*) both swims and walks around its habitat of well vegetated fresh water over which it builds a bulky, cup shaped nest.

The more solitary eastern great egret (*Ardea modesta*) can be seen wading through water bodies where it fishes, while the black bittern (*Dupetor flavicollis*) is a bird seldom seen owing to its secretive and solitary nature as well as its crepuscular habits.

Baillon's crake (*Porzana pusilla*) is another secretive bird, skulking in marshy vegetation and reed beds yet visible when it comes out to feed on muddy areas. The swamp francolin (*Francolinus gularis*) likes the water yet spends much of its time on nearby land often concealed within tall, wet grassland.

The Pacific golden plover (*Pluvialis fulva*) may be seen roosting on the coast but flies to grassy areas to feed on insects as well as beetles and earthworms. The much smaller moustached warbler (*Acrocephalus melanopogon*) can be seen hopping around vegetation over water although much of the time it remains hidden from the view.

There is an increasing tendency for swamps to be drained to make them more productive areas of land; in doing so, many birds are deprived of their natural habitats.

An endangered adult male greater adjutant stork (*Leptoptilos dubius*) stands at the egde of a pond in Guwahati, Assam.

(*Previous pages*) A sarus crane (*Grus antigone*) runs back to its calling mate over waterlogged ground in Rajasthan.

A female western marsh harrier (*Circus aeruginosus*) perches on a vantage point where it can see the surrounding area.

(*Opposite*) A greater spotted eagle (*Aquila clanga*) perches on a thorn bush while hunting prey amidst the marshes of the Banni Grasslands of Gujarat.

A purple swamphen (*Porphyrio porphyrio*) at home among the marshes of Rajasthan.

(*Opposite*) A white-breasted waterhen (*Amaurornis phoenicurus*) walks nimbly through the Osho Teerth Park in Pune, Maharashtra.

An eastern great egret (*Ardea modesta*) perches on a tree in the Keoladeo National Park where the monsoon rains have turned the surrounding area into a swamp.

A black bittern (*Dupetor flavicollis*) makes a brief appearance at the edge of a dyke near the main tourist route through Keoladeo National Park.

A Baillon's crake (*Porzana pusilla*) amidst undergrowth bordering the Yamuna River.

(*Opposite*) A pair of swamp francolin (*Francolinus gularis*) crossing the wet grassland of Kaziranga National Park.

By the Yamuna River, a moustached warbler (*Acrocephalus melanopogon*) can be seen for a moment or two atop rotting vegetation.

(*Opposite*) A Pacific golden plover (*Pluvialis fulva*) wades through a large puddle near the coast.

BIRDS OF THE GRASSLAND

Grassland is where a great variety of grass species is the predominant vegetation.

Grassland is an area of land covered largely by grass where herbaceous plants, shrubs and some trees may also be found.

The white stork (*Ciconia ciconia*) found in moister environments, feeds in grasslands, sometimes following mammals as well as fires since both disturb insects and make them an easier prey.

The often solitary and endangered Bengal florican (*Houbaropsis benghalensis*) is not easy to observe since it hides amidst the grasses, usually visible only when emerging into shorter grassland or when displaying during the breeding season; omnivorous, it eats mostly invertebrates and vegetable matter.

The short-eared owl (*Asio flammeus*) has similar hunting habits being more diurnal than other owls; when not hunting, the bird usually roosts on the ground. The pied harrier (*Circus melanoleucos*) is seen flying low and leisurely over grassland as it hunts prey such as rodents, frogs, small birds and larger insects; these harriers can sometimes be seen hunting together.

The striated grassbird (*Megalurus palustris*) is attracted to grassland near water and nests in reeds, building a rough structure from coarse grasses, while the much larger common crane (*Grus grus*) often roosts in marshland at night, flying out to grassland during the day to feed.

The Siberian stonechat (*Saxicola maurus*) frequents a number of different environments yet likes grassland for here it can find low vegetation from which it makes forays for the invertebrates it feeds on, while the zitting cisticola (*Cisticola juncidis*) inhabits grasses of different kinds in which it builds a pouch-shaped nest suspended between grass stems.

Yellow-bellied prinia (*Prinia flaviventris*) likes tall grassland often near water and builds an oval nest of fine grass on grass stems or in bushes. The booted warbler (*Hippolais caligata*) breeds in areas near water yet in the winter prefers drier habitats such as deciduous scrub, bushes on the edge of cultivation, grass clumps and acacias.

Weavers are a group of birds that favour open areas of grassland. The black-breasted weaver (*Ploceus benghalensis*) likes tall, damp, seasonally flooded grassland while the baya weaver (*Ploceus philippinus*) favours a wider variety of habitats often constructing its suspended retort-shaped nest near or even over water.

Grasslands are sometimes wild and at other times under cultivation by humans. In the latter case, the use of chemicals can destroy the food chain of birds who often live off insects harmful to crops and other creatures while wild grasslands are shrinking, as the demands of man on the environment increase.

A Bengal florican (*Houbaropsis benghalensis*) in grassland bordering the edge of Manas National Park.

(*Previous pages*) A white stork (*Ciconia ciconia*) forages on grassland in Gujarat.

49

A short-eared owl (*Asio flammeus*) roosting during the day in the grasses of Gujarat.

A young pied harrier (*Circus melanoleucos*) in grassland near the Manas National Park.

A striated grassbird
(*Megalurus palustris*)
calls from the
top of a reed.

(*Opposite*)
A common crane
(*Grus grus*)
calls while flying
over the grasslands
of Gujarat.

A Siberian stonechat (*Saxicola maurus*) hangs to the branch of a bush from where it can make short forays to catch insects.

(*Opposite*) A zitting cisticola (*Cisticola juncidis*) clings to a stem in a grassland.

A yellow-bellied prinia (*Prinia flaviventris*) among reeds beside the Yamuna River.

A booted warbler (*Hippolais caligata*) amidst vegetation bordering the Yamuna River.

A baya weaver (*Ploceus philippinus)* perches
for a moment or two upon a spreading leaf.

(*Opposite*) A black-breasted weaver (*Ploceus benghalensis*) clings to a dried reed.

BIRDS OF THE SCRUB

Even apparently useless ground can be of value to birds.

Scrub is a term used here to describe land that is of inferior quality and often arid yet of considerable value to birds; it may support thick even impenetrable vegetation but the soil is generally not suitable for growing crops and in some cases is sandy.

A bird such as the grey francolin (*Francolinus pondicerianus*) likes a number of habitats of which scrub is a favourite, for here the ground can be easily scratched to procure a diet of seeds and insects while adequate cover may be found when required.

One bird typically found inhabiting such an environment is the short-toed snake eagle (*Circaetus gallicus*) as it soars and hovers in the search for prey, plummeting down to nimbly catch its preferred diet of snake with its claws before eventually killing it with the beak.

The laughing dove (*Streptopelia senegalensis*) is not a shy bird and can be found close to human habitation yet has a liking for dry open habitats particularly where cacti grow. While there are many different species of babbler, the common babbler (*Turdoides caudata*) which may visit gardens, can be seen hopping along the ground even scuttling as it disappears under vegetation, groups keeping up a conversation of squeaks, trills and whistles as they go.

The Indian bushlark (*Mirafra erythroptera*) is fond of bushes such as *Euphorbia* on the tops of which it can be seen perching; while the white-eared bulbul (*Pycnonotus leucotis*) also seen in gardens, feeds on fruit and invertebrates, caught on the ground and in the air.

The lesser whitethroat (*Sylvia curruca*) tends to keep well hidden while foraging in trees and bushes that grow in drier areas; while the isabelline or rufous-tailed shrike (*Lanius isabellinus*) like the drier, open, uncultivated areas where they feed mostly on large insects.

The ashy prinia (*Prinia socialis*) is usually found low down in vegetation in a wide variety of habitats some of which are near water. The sulphur-bellied warbler (*Phylloscopus griseolus*) likes rocky areas where there is a certain amount of vegetation.

Scrub is an area often left undisturbed by the populace who see hardly any value in its presence. With little understanding of the importance these areas contribute to the general ecological balance, man's expansion continues largely unhindered and the many different species areas of scrub support now face a common threat to their livelihood.

A short-toed snake eagle (*Circaetus gallicus*) on top a dead tree surveying the surrounding area for possible prey.

(*Previous pages*) A grey francolin (*Francolinus pondicerianus*) in the scrubland of Tal Chhapar Wildlife Sanctuary, Rajasthan.

A group of common babbler (*Turdoides caudata*) in a patch of scrubland amidst rocky hills near Jaisalmer in Rajasthan.

(*Opposite*) A laughing dove (*Streptopelia senegalensis*) in the gardens of the India International Centre, New Delhi.

A lesser whitethroat (*Sylvia curruca*) perches in a bush virtually invisible to a passer by.

(66) An Indian bushlark (*Mirafra erythroptera*) atop a bush in Kutch, Gujarat.
(67) A white-eared bulbul (*Pycnonotus leucotis*) perches by a roadside in Rajasthan.

An isabelline shrike (*Lanius isabellinus*) on the outskirts of Gurgaon.

A sulphur-bellied warbler (*Phylloscopus griseolus*) in the scrub adjoining a dried river bed in the Morni hills in northern Haryana.

(*Opposite*) An ashy prinia (*Prinia socialis*) calls from a thorny bush.

BIRDS OF THE DESERT

Deserts are areas of harsh and dry climatic conditions
yet can be surprisingly rich in biodiversity.

The desert regions of the Indian subcontinent contain areas of rolling dunes and salt flats; they are extremely arid regions with little or no vegetation, the land surface being typically sandy or rocky with a minimum amount of soil cover. Desert regions are found in Rajasthan, India and southern Pakistan while there are also montane deserts such as those of Mustang in the Nepalese Himalaya.

The tawny eagle (*Aquila rapax*) is found in desert regions yet likes a certain amount of vegetation such as a tree to nest in or hunt from. This eagle has a varied diet consisting of carrion and refuse; small mammals are caught by pouncing on them from a low bush or stolen from other birds of prey while it will also consume other birds and reptiles.

The griffon vulture (*Gyps fulvus*) is skilled at soaring and gliding, sometimes for long distances before coming to ground where a carcass is to be found.

The southern grey shrike (*Lanius meridionalis*) likes dry areas such as the semi-desert or thorn scrub; it is a wary and aggressive member of the shrike family that characteristically appropriates the nests of other birds. The desert wheatear (*Oenanthe deserti*) frequents desert areas of rock or sand with scattered bushes such as *Caragana* but can be found on ploughed and fallow land in irrigated areas; it hunts insects particularly beetles from above and by hopping along the ground.

The desert lark (*Ammomanes deserti*) lives up to its name in preferring arid habitats such as rocky foothills and ravines yet may be found on the fallow land of desert-canal cultivation; it perches on rocks and feeds on seeds and insects. The trumpeter finch (*Bucanetes githagineus*) can likewise be found in drier areas such as the stony semi-desert and dry rocky hills. It is prepared to fly some distance for water.

Deserts are not areas that humans can easily inhabit and exploit owing to the harshness of the environment hence bird life is not so threatened, yet neither is it so densely populated as other habitats.

A griffon vulture (*Gyps fulvus*) near a roadside kill south of Jaisalmer.

(*Previous pages*) An immature tawny eagle (*Aquila rapax*) perches on a tree in the Desert National Park, Rajasthan.

A desert wheatear (*Oenanthe deserti*) stands alert.

(*Opposite*) A southern grey shrike (*Lanius meridionalis*) perches on a stone.

A desert lark (*Ammomanes deserti*) among stones in a desert near Jaisalmer.

A trumpeter finch (*Bucanetes githagineus*) wintering around a rocky outcrop near Jaisalmer.

BIRDS
OF THE
WOODS

A wood is an area of land
dominated by trees and a
forest is formed when
there is significant
canopy overhead.

Birds are naturally attracted to trees as they provide shelter, support and also food particularly when covered in foliage. There are many different kinds of woods or forests in the Indian subcontinent and variations in tree types inevitably account for different kinds of birds as do factors such as the density of the overlying canopy and the altitude.

The often wary, near threatened great hornbill (*Buceros bicornis*), a bird of mature broadleaved evergreen and moist deciduous forests, can be seen amidst the higher canopy where it spends much of its time, living on fruit, nestlings and reptiles, descending occasionally to feed.

The crested serpent eagle (*Spilornis cheela*) roosts upright within foliage inhabiting deciduous and moist evergreen forests above which it can be seen soaring; it likes to be near water and hunts snakes, not its only prey, dropping down on them from a perch.

The dusky eagle-owl (*Bubo coromandus*) can be found in well-watered areas with a variety of woodland including trees alongside roads and near villages; it feeds on birds and mammals. The shikra (*Accipiter badius*) hunts in more open country with lighter woodland often close to habitation, flying quickly to capture a variety of smaller birds, mammals, reptiles and insects.

Especially fond of figs, the blue-throated barbet (*Megalaima asiatica*) likes a number of different wooded habitats, both deciduous and evergreen, nesting in trees by digging a hole; it is also found in gardens as is the Asian koel (*Eudynamys scolopaceus*) which is often hard to see as it keeps well hidden while calling loudly yet occasionally. Sometimes it can be seen sunning itself or flying hurriedly between trees with a strong and direct flight; it feeds on fruit, berries and insects.

The grey-headed woodpecker (*Picus canus*) is found in mixed conifer and broadleaved forests feeding on the ground for ants and termites although it will also occasionally eat fruit and nectar. The greater goldenback (*Chrysocolaptes lucidus*) is usually found below 1000 meters in broadleaved forests, coffee plantations and mangroves; it forages at all levels especially on dead wood.

Another bird of the woods that is also found in hilly areas is the chestnut-bellied nuthatch (*Sitta cinnamoventris*); it can be seen clawing its way up tree trunks as it searches for spiders, grubs and insects amidst the crevices formed on the tree bark. The brown-breasted flycatcher (*Muscicapa muttui*) is a small, solitary bird inhabiting the thickets and tangles of broadleaved evergreen forests where it can be found in the lower canopy.

Woodland offers birds protection from many predators yet the chainsaw is a new menace and as forests are disappearing at an alarming rate, many birds will find it difficult even impossible to find alternative habitats.

In the sun of a winter morning, a crested serpent eagle (*Spilornis cheela*) warms itself at Keoladeo National Park.

(*Previous pages*) A group of great hornbill (*Buceros bicornis*) rest for a while in the canopy of an Assamese tea garden.

A dusky eagle-owl (*Bubo coromandus*) adult with chick
at Keoladeo National Park.

(*Opposite*) An immature shikra (*Accipiter badius*) at Sultanpur National Park, Haryana.

A female Asian koel (*Eudynamys scolopaceus*)
in the trees of a modern city suburb.

A blue-throated barbet (*Megalaima asiatica*)
in the woods of the Tollygunge Club, Kolkata.

A grey-headed woodpecker (*Picus canus*) in an Assamese tea garden.

(*Opposite*)
A greater goldenback
(*Chrysocolaptes lucidus*)
in the forests of the
Western Ghats.

Brown-breasted flycatcher (*Muscicapa muttui*)
in the woods of Bhagwan Mahavir Wildlife Sanctuary, Goa.

(*Opposite*) A female chestnut-bellied nuthatch (*Sitta cinnamoventris*) above a nest hole in Uttarakhand.

BIRDS OF THE MOUNTAINS

Mountains are areas of high ground giving rise to a unique kind of wildlife.

The mountainous area of the Indian sub continent known as the Himalayas is rich in bird life. Although covering only about 10 percent of the area, it contains a unique and varied collection of birds in which more than 50 percent of the region's species are to be found. There are also the bird rich Western Ghats. The actual height of the slopes is important in determining the occurrence of different bird species; owing to forested slopes, many can be considered woodland species.

Often eagles are fond of the mountains and the black eagle (*Ictinaetus malayensis*) is one of these; it can be seen soaring and gliding over the moist-deciduous and evergreen forests it favours. The forest dwelling, rufous-necked hornbill (*Aceros nipalensis*) is found in hills of the north-east up to a height of about 2000 metres.

The noisy and gregarious slaty-headed parakeet (*Psittacula himalayana*) is a member of the populous parakeet family and found in the mountains where it feeds on seeds, fruits, blossoms and leaf buds. The speckled wood pigeon (*Columba hodgsonii*) can be observed at the edge of forests, typically on a bare emergent branch; it does however, visit other habitats such as scrub.

There are a number of thrush and blackbird species found in the Himalayas, one of which is the white-collared blackbird (*Turdus albocinctus*) often seen at the fringes of woodland. The great barbet (*Megalaima virens*) can often be heard calling in the hills and may descend to lower altitudes in winter; it is also found in wooded areas.

The rufous sibia (*Heterophasia capistrata*) forages through the foliage of different kinds of woodland such as oak and pine, in search of insects, berries and plant nectars. The blue-capped rock thrush (*Monticola cinclorhynchus*) during summer is found in open dry forest or dry rocky slopes with scattered trees while in winter, it inhabits deciduous forest. It can be found in the Himalayas during the summer months and the Ghats during the winter months.

Among the bulbuls with affinity towards mountains, Himalayan bulbul (*Pycnonotus leucogenys*) can be seen in wooded areas and may descend to the plains in winter; it has a boisterous nature and is conspicuous when it perches on the tops of bushes, flicking its wings and tail. The rather shy mountain bulbul (*Ixos mcclellandii*) is a bird that frequents various mountainous habitats and can be seen in the higher canopy, feeding largely on berries and fruits.

The plumbeous water redstart (*Rhyacornis fuliginosa*) is a common bird near fast flowing mountain streams and rivers often moving to larger water bodies during the winter months. The brown dipper (*Cinclus pallasii*) however is a bird usually seen at the water's edge of shallow rapids and rivers as well as small mountain lakes.

Mountains are often remote areas that can act as a repository for birds that are no longer able to survive elsewhere. However, the modern world still adversely effects them as trees are felled and rain carries pollutants.

An adult male rufous-necked hornbill (*Aceros nipalensis*) at Eagle's Nest in Arunachal Pradesh.

(*Previous pages*) A black eagle (*Ictinaetus malayensis*) above a valley north of Kathmandu, Nepal.

A speckled wood pigeon (*Columba hodgsonii*)
in the Himalayan valley of Munsiyari, Uttarakhand.

(*Opposite*) A slaty-headed parakeet (*Psittacula himalayana*)
in forested slopes below the Kedarnath Wildlife Sanctuary, Uttarakhand.

A male white-collared blackbird (*Turdus albocinctus*) in the eastern Himalayas.

(*Opposite*) A great barbet (*Megalaima virens*) near Dharamshala, Himachal Pradesh.

(*Opposite*) A rufous sibia (*Heterophasia capistrata*) on the slopes
of Phulchowki hill, Kathmandu valley, Nepal.

A blue-capped rock thrush (*Monticola cinclorhynchus*) in the forests of Bondla Wildlife Sanctuary, Goa.

A Himalayan bulbul (*Pycnonotus leucogenys*) in the Morni hills.

A mountain bulbul (*Ixos mcclellandii*) in a forest near Kathmandu.

Plumbeous water redstart (*Rhyacornis fuligonosis*)
on a rock near the entrance to the Shivpuri National Park, Nepal.

(*Opposite*) Brown dipper (*Cinclus pallasii*) beside a mountain stream
near Dehradun, Uttarakhand.

BIRDS OF HUMAN HABITATION

A black kite (*Milvus migrans*) soaks up the winter sunshine
beside the ring road in South Delhi.

Many wild birds are attracted to human habitation since man's activities can make the opportunity of finding food that much easier, as well as providing both roosting and nesting possibilities. The relationship is of mutual benefit, for birds can often play an important role in keeping insect populations under control while some birds will take vermin such as rats. To farmers, birds are a mixed blessing for while they eat the insects that might otherwise damage crops, they also eat the crops themselves. One example of this competition of resources is the coastal dwelling western reef heron (*Egretta gularis*) that pirates fish from nets.

The black kite (*Milvus migrans*) can be seen by the dozen occasionally even in their hundreds, around many of the region's major cities where they feed off rubbish, vermin and carrion as well as snatching food meant for humans, being adroit flyers capable of manoeuvring around buildings and telephone wires.

The delicate chirping calls of the house sparrow (*Passer domesticus*) can sometimes be heard close to home, although modern housing seldom considers nesting and other bird's needs which accounts for a significant drop in the numbers of such birds as they struggle to find appropriate places to build nests.

The common pigeon (*Columba livia*) has been known to man for thousands of years being mentioned in an ancient text, the *Rig Veda*, and can usually be seen in large flocks near and perching on buildings, it still does occasionally nest in its original habitat of cliff faces and rocks.

The western barn owl (*Tyto alba*) is often found in the vicinity of human habitation being a bird that likes old buildings; it is seldom seen however owing to its nocturnal habits. The noisy rose-ringed parakeet (*Psittacula krameri*) calling as it flies, can often be seen in the vicinity of gardens and parks; it is considered a pest as it is one of a number of birds that feed on crops such as cultivated fruits and grains and is also partial to flowers, both nectar and petals. It nests in holes found in buildings as well as those in trees and cliffs.

Birds and humans have been in a relationship for ages and it seems set to continue. Birds are adapting to the challenges of modern urban growth while human knowledge and understanding of avian life steadily increases. In today's world, the presence of Nature is no longer taken so much for granted and the need to coexist is becoming an urgent reality.

(*Previous pages*) Birds can sometimes be a pest to man such as these western reef heron (*Egretta gularis*) using fisherman's nets to help catch their prey.

A female house sparrow (*Passer domesticus*) looks for possible nesting space;
lack of suitable places particularly in predominately concrete cities has lead to a decline in the bird's numbers.

(*Opposite*) A not uncommon sight near human habitation;
a common pigeon (*Columba livia*) perching on a roof top.

A pair of western barn owl (*Tyto alba*)
roost overnight at a church in Goa.

(*Opposite*) A pair of rose-ringed parakeet (*Psittacula krameri*) chicks
in a nest hole facing the Norbulingka Institute, Dharamshala.

AFTERWORD

Often, it is where two or more habitat types merge that birds are found; this further hinders the general classification of birds according to a particular environment. Nevertheless, this does not invalidate the importance of environmental factors when trying to understand the characteristics of birds while working towards their welfare.

Some birds have their preferred habitat mentioned in their name such as with the swamp francolin, yet names can be misleading. For instance, the name "common moorhen" is archaic and might really be better called "common waterhen" for here, the term "moor" is a derivation of "mere", the French for water.

A particular family of birds is likely to have similar but not the same kind of habitat. The three crane species mentioned in this book are all found in different environments with the demoiselle crane being a bird attracted to the waterside, the sarus crane to the swamp and the common crane to grassland. Yet the relative proximity of water is a common feature for all of them as it is for the black-necked crane (*Grus nigricollis*), a bird of the mountains, that is found nesting on bogs and marshes while it spends winters in wetlands and fields.

The threat to the avian population in the Indian subcontinent today as elsewhere on the planet, is largely a result of the destruction of their natural environment not just by the excessive demands of a burgeoning human population but also the increasing and far reaching influence of climate change; it remains to be seen how well both birds and man will respond to these challenges. The importance of the relationship between the environment and birds cannot be understated for without suitable places to inhabit, many birds would soon become extinct just as many are already threatened.

By helping to maintain appropriate environments, we can help enable birds to survive into an uncertain future as well as make a positive contribution to our own questionable foundations.

The wallcreeper (*Tichodroma muraria*) is an example of a bird that has exploited a particular micro-environment; it feeds on spiders and other invertebrates from vertical rockfaces where it builds its mossy nest.

INDEX of ENGLISH BIRD NAMES followed by Hindi names.

INDEX of SCIENTIFIC BIRD NAMES followed by size in centimetres.

REFERENCES

Birds in Sanskrit Literature by K.N.Dave
(Motilal Banarasidas 1985)

Birds of the Indian Subcontinent by Carol Inskipp, Richard Grimmett and Tim Inskipp
(Helm Identification Guides 1998)

Birds of South Asia: The Ripley Guide by Pamela C. Rasmussen and John C. Anderton
(Smithsonian Institution 2005)

A Field Guide to the Birds of India by Krys Kazmierczak
(OM Book Service 2000)

Birds of the World (Recommended English Names) by Frank Gill and Minturn Wright
(Christopher Helm 2006)

The 2006 IUCN Red List of Threatened Species

ACKNOWLEDGEMENTS

My thanks to Maan Barua of Kaziranga, Assam for discussing the concept of this book with me and also Shobit Arya of Wisdom Tree India for encouraging its development. Support also came from the itinerant band of Indian birders both local and foreign who help to keep awareness of birds and their needs alive in the Indian subcontinent. Special thanks to the staff of Wisdom Tree.

PHOTOGRAPHY

The photographs in this book, all from within the Indian subcontinent, were made using a digital SLR camera with a supported telephoto lens. Images were downloaded and written to disc before being opened in image editing software where the brightness, contrast and colour were adjusted to print natural looking and reasonably accurate photographs; the only photomontage is of the black eagle pasted onto a landscape view with both images being made within a short time and distance of each other. Photographs were sized, sharpened and loaded into a desktop publishing programme where text was then added, making the book ready for plate making and printing.

INDEX

Sizes are taken from the Inskipp, Grimmett and Inskipp book mentioned above; bird names are based on the International Ornithological Conference's most recent available update.